discover more

Exploring Life Science

Living and Nonliving Things

Ernest Brazzos

Britannica Educational Publishing

IN ASSOCIATION WITH

THE ROSEN PUBLISHING GROUP

Published in 2025 by The Rosen Publishing Group, Inc.
2544 Clinton Street, Buffalo, NY 14224

Editor: Brianna Propis
Book Design: Michael Flynn

Photo Credits: Cover Txema Gerardo/Shutterstock.com; (series background) Dai Yim/Shutterstock.com; p. 4 Prostock-studio/Shutterstock.com; p. 5 Jacek Chabraszewski/Shutterstock.com; p. 6 colacat/Shutterstock.com; p. 7 SIM ONE/Shutterstock.com; p. 9 (top) EsHanPhot/Shutterstock.com; p. 9 (bottom) Natalia Golovina/Shutterstock.com; p. 11 Valmedia/Shutterstock.com; p. 13 (top) Reddogs/Shutterstock.com; p. 13 (bottom) W. de Vries/Shutterstock.com; p. 14 Phonlamai Photo/Shutterstock.com; p. 15 Henk Bogaard/Shutterstock.com; p. 17 FJAH/Shutterstock.com; p. 18 Juris Kraulis/Shutterstock.com; p. 19 Krakenimages.com/Shutterstock.com; p. 20 IgorCheri/Shutterstock.com; p. 21 Matt Jeppson/Shutterstock.com; p. 22 Sergevna/Shutterstock.com; p. 23 JPRFPhotos/Shutterstock.com; p. 24 paulista/Shutterstock.com; p. 25 BlueRingMedia/Shutterstock.com; p. 26 bunyiam/Shutterstock.com; p. 27 MikroKon/Shutterstock.com; p. 29 Studio Romantic/Shutterstock.com; p. 29 OlgaKhorkova/Shutterstock.com.

Library of Congress Cataloging-in-Publication Data

Names: Brazzos, Ernest, author.
Title: Living and nonliving things / Ernest Brazzos.
Description: [Buffalo] : Britannica Educational Publishing, [2025] | Series: Discover more! Exploring life science | Includes bibliographical references and index.
Identifiers: LCCN 2023051696 (print) | LCCN 2023051697 (ebook) | ISBN 9781641901680 (library binding) | ISBN 9781641901673 (paperback) | ISBN 9781641901697 (ebook)
Subjects: LCSH: Life (Biology)--Juvenile literature.
Classification: LCC QH501 .B763 2025 (print) | LCC QH501 (ebook) | DDC 570--dc23/eng/20231214
LC record available at https://lccn.loc.gov/2023051696
LC ebook record available at https://lccn.loc.gov/2023051697

Manufactured in the United States of America

Some of the images in this book illustrate individuals who are models. The depictions do not imply actual situations or events.

CPSIA Compliance Information: Batch #CSBRIT25. For further information contact Rosen Publishing at 1-800-237-9932.

Contents

The World Around Us

Imagine walking in the park on a sunny day. You might see many living things, such as people, dogs, plants, insects, and birds. You might also see nonliving things, such as roads, benches, and ponds. Living things need food and water to live, but nonliving things do not.

You, your family, and your pet are all living things.

Living and nonliving things have different purposes in the world. Which of the things in the picture are living, and which are nonliving?

Sometimes living and nonliving things can look and feel very similar. For example, living things can move, but so can some nonliving things, such as cars and waves. Rocks aren't alive, but some rocks, called crystals, grow like living plants. What's one way to tell if something is living or nonliving?

Consider This

Think of the living and nonliving things in your home or outside. Can you find any nonliving things made from living things?

It's Alive!

A furry bumblebee, a giant redwood tree, a slimy frog, and a purple tulip all look completely different. We can tell they're living things because they all carry out seven **life processes**. These are special abilities that allow living things to survive. Only a living thing can carry out these processes.

Eating food is necessary to survive. It is one of the seven life processes.

Lithops are succulents, a type of plant that looks like stones. However, we know they are alive because they carry out all seven life processes.

You can remember the life processes by taking the first letter of each word to make the name "Mrs. Gren":

Movement: the act of moving

Reproduction: the process of producing new living things

Sensitivity: the ability to respond to physical information

Growth: the process of getting bigger

Respiration: a chemical reaction that produces energy

Excretion: the process of getting rid of waste

Nutrition: the result of taking in and making use of food

WORD WISE

A LIFE PROCESS IS AN ACTION THAT LIVING THINGS MUST DO TO SURVIVE.

Let's Get Moving

Movement is one of the seven life processes that living things can do. People and animals move to get food, to find partners with whom to have young, and to escape danger. Living things move in different ways.

Plants usually stay in one place, but they move as they grow and become taller. Plants need sunlight to grow, so their leaves or flowers will turn to face the sun.

Different animals have unique body parts that help them move in different ways. Monkeys have long arms and fingers so they can swing between branches in a forest. Sharks and fish move their tails up and down to swim in the ocean.

The Venus flytrap catches flies by shutting its leaves quickly when one lands on it.

compare**and**contrast

Fish move by swimming, and birds move by flying. Which body parts do they use to make them move, and how do they move them?

A giraffe's legs are taller than many humans–they're 6 feet (1.8 m) long! Their long legs allow them to run as fast as 35 miles (56 km) per hour.

Eat to Live

Eating nutrients, or food, is necessary for the survival of living things. Animals eat the food they need. Plants make their own food by **photosynthesis**. They use sunlight to turn water and **carbon dioxide** into food. Plants use this food to live and grow. Some animals eat certain plants for sustenance, which is food that helps them live and grow!

The animals that eat plants are eaten by other animals. Zebras eat grass and then lions eat the zebras. Mice eat seeds and then foxes eat the mice. Chickens eat grass and then humans cook and eat the chicken.

Consider This

Can you think of another animal that people eat that feeds on plants?

WORD WISE

PHOTOSYNTHESIS IS THE PROCESS PLANTS USE TO TURN SUNLIGHT INTO FOOD.

Snakes open their jaws wide to swallow prey whole!

WORD WISE

CARBON DIOXIDE IS A GAS FOUND IN THE AIR THAT PLANTS TURN INTO OXYGEN.

Keep Breathing

A living thing must release energy in order to use food. All living things need energy to grow, move, and carry out other life processes. Living things release energy from food by respiration, or breathing.

Respiration happens throughout the body of a living thing when sugars from food combine with oxygen. Oxygen is a gas in the air. Most animals take in air through their mouths and noses.

Other living things breathe and receive oxygen for respiration differently. Oxygen is sometimes hard for birds to find high in the air, so they have many air sacs in their bodies to help them breathe—including in their rear ends!

On the other hand, most plants take in carbon dioxide from the air through tiny holes, called stomata, on their leaves. They release oxygen through the same holes.

Dogs can't sweat like humans do. They pant to breathe in oxygen as well as to cool their bodies down.

compare and contrast

Cars won't move unless they have fuel in the engines. Electronic devices won't turn on unless they're charged. How is food like fuel, or like a charge, for living things?

Fish and newts take in oxygen from water using special body parts called gills.

Waste

Waste is created as a result of the seven life processes. Waste can be harmful if it builds up inside living things. Excretion is the way the body gets rid of waste. During respiration, animals produce waste as a gas called carbon dioxide. It's often breathed out of their mouths and noses.

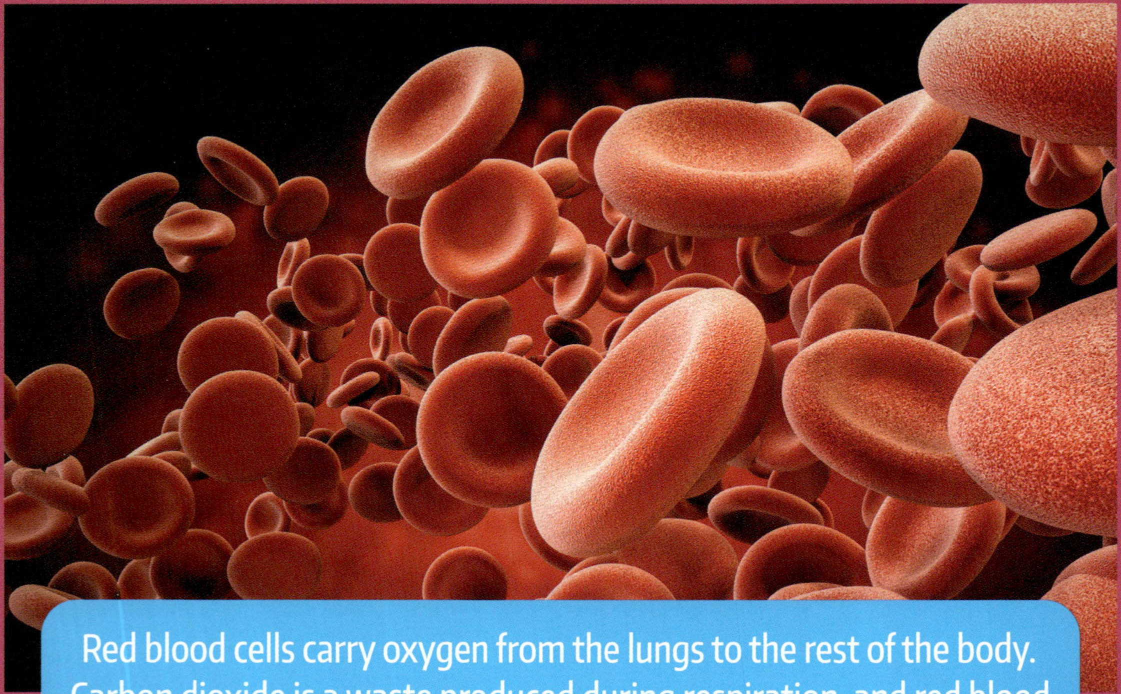

Red blood cells carry oxygen from the lungs to the rest of the body. Carbon dioxide is a waste produced during respiration, and red blood cells carry it back to the lungs to be exhaled.

The world would be covered in waste were it not for decomposers, or creatures that feed on dead materials and waste. Dung beetles eat feces and lay their eggs inside it.

A lot of waste comes from food. Trees get rid of their food waste, oxygen, through their leaves. Humans and animals excrete urine and feces to remove extra water and food waste from their bodies.

Consider This

Oxygen, produced by plants, is necessary for living things to breathe in and live out their life functions. Why is it important for us to care for the environment and protect plant life?

Sensible

Living things need sense to be able to react to the world and environments around them. Senses include touch, sight, hearing, smell, and taste. Animals use senses to find food and other animals to have young with, and to escape danger. For example, deer need a strong sense of hearing and eyesight to detect an approaching **predator**, such as a wolf.

Living things use their senses in unique ways to help them move. Tips of plant roots sense which way is down so they grow into the soil. Catfish have whisker-like feelers to find food. A scorpion has tiny hairs on its pincers that feel air movements, which helps them find **prey**.

compare and contrast

How might humans and animals use their senses differently depending on the time of day?

WORD WISE

PREY IS AN ANIMAL HUNTED BY ANOTHER ANIMAL. PREDATOR IS AN ANIMAL THAT HUNTS AND KILLS OTHER ANIMALS FOR FOOD.

Nocturnal animals, or animals that are most active at night, have strong senses of hearing, smell, and eyesight so they can move in darkness.

New Life

All living things create new life through reproduction, the process of producing babies that look like their parents. Most plants reproduce by growing seeds from their flowers. When the seeds fall or blow away from the plant and land in dirt, they grow into a new plant. Some animals, such as birds and reptiles, lay eggs. Their babies develop inside the eggs until they're ready to hatch.

Bird eggs have a hard shell, while most reptile eggs are softer.

Human mothers grow their babies inside their bodies for nine months before giving birth.

Mammals, such as dogs, dolphins, and humans, are animals that give live birth, or have babies develop inside the mother's body. Marsupial mammals, such as kangaroos, have tiny babies that must spend a long time in their mother's pouch before they're able to survive in the outside world. Dolphins, whales, and manatees are the only mammals that spend their entire lives underwater.

Growth and Change

As living things grow, their bodies create new parts and materials and change old ones. This happens when a seed grows into a plant, or a chick grows into a hen. As humans grow, they add new parts, such as teeth, and change the size of others, such as their ears, nose, hair, and nails.

Tree trunks keep growing wider and add new rings year after year.

Some lizards, such as iguanas and geckos, can regrow their tails if they fall off.

Living things have a special kind of growth that heals injuries. Shrubs and trees mend injuries by covering them with bark. Human bodies can heal scraped skin and mend broken bones.

Life and Death

All livings things die at some point in their lives. They stay alive as long as they can carry out the life processes. Once the life processes stop, they die. Some plants die if they don't get enough water or sunlight because then they can't make the food they need. Animals such as bears may die if their bodies are injured, and they can't move to catch food.

Living things must drink water to stay alive.

When living things reach the end of their natural life, their life processes slow down and, finally, stop. As living things get old, the parts that help them grow, feed, move, and breathe start to wear out. At some point, they will die.

Consider This

What would happen if animals and plants no longer reproduced and stopped bringing offspring into the world?

Grouping Together

Living things have the seven life processes in common, but they can still be very different from one another. To help us understand and study living things, we can group them. The main ways they're grouped are based on the similarities and differences in the ways living things carry out life processes, and by the number of **cells** in their bodies.

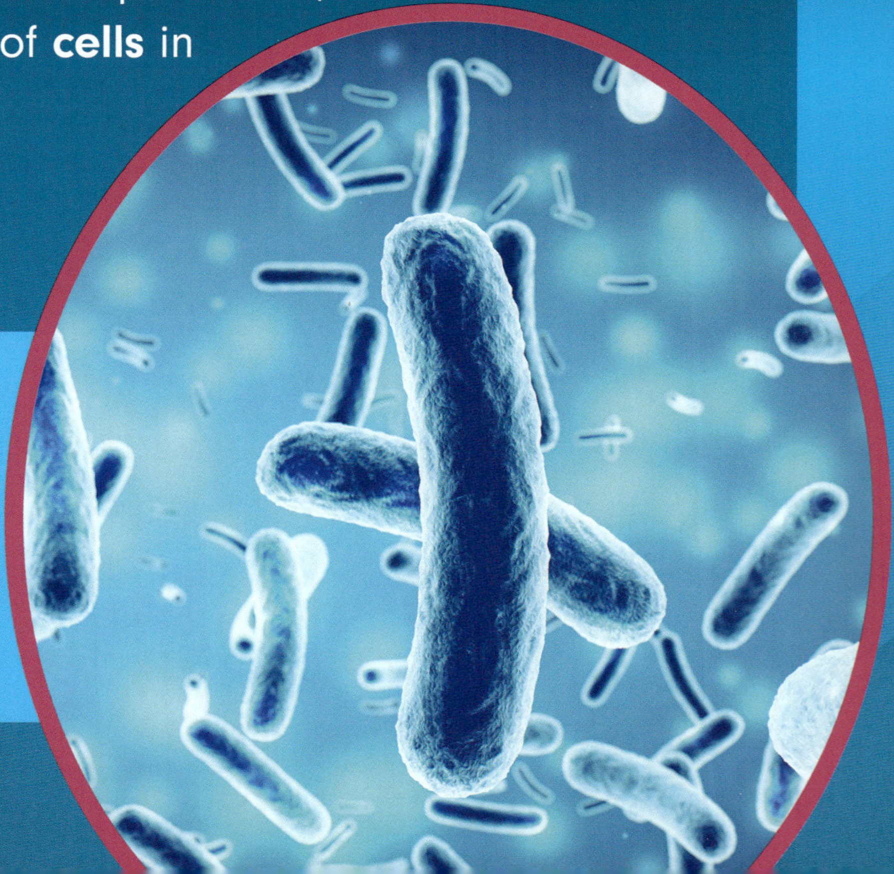

Bacteria are small, single-celled living things. Infectious, or easily transmitted, bacteria can make you ill if they reproduce inside your body.

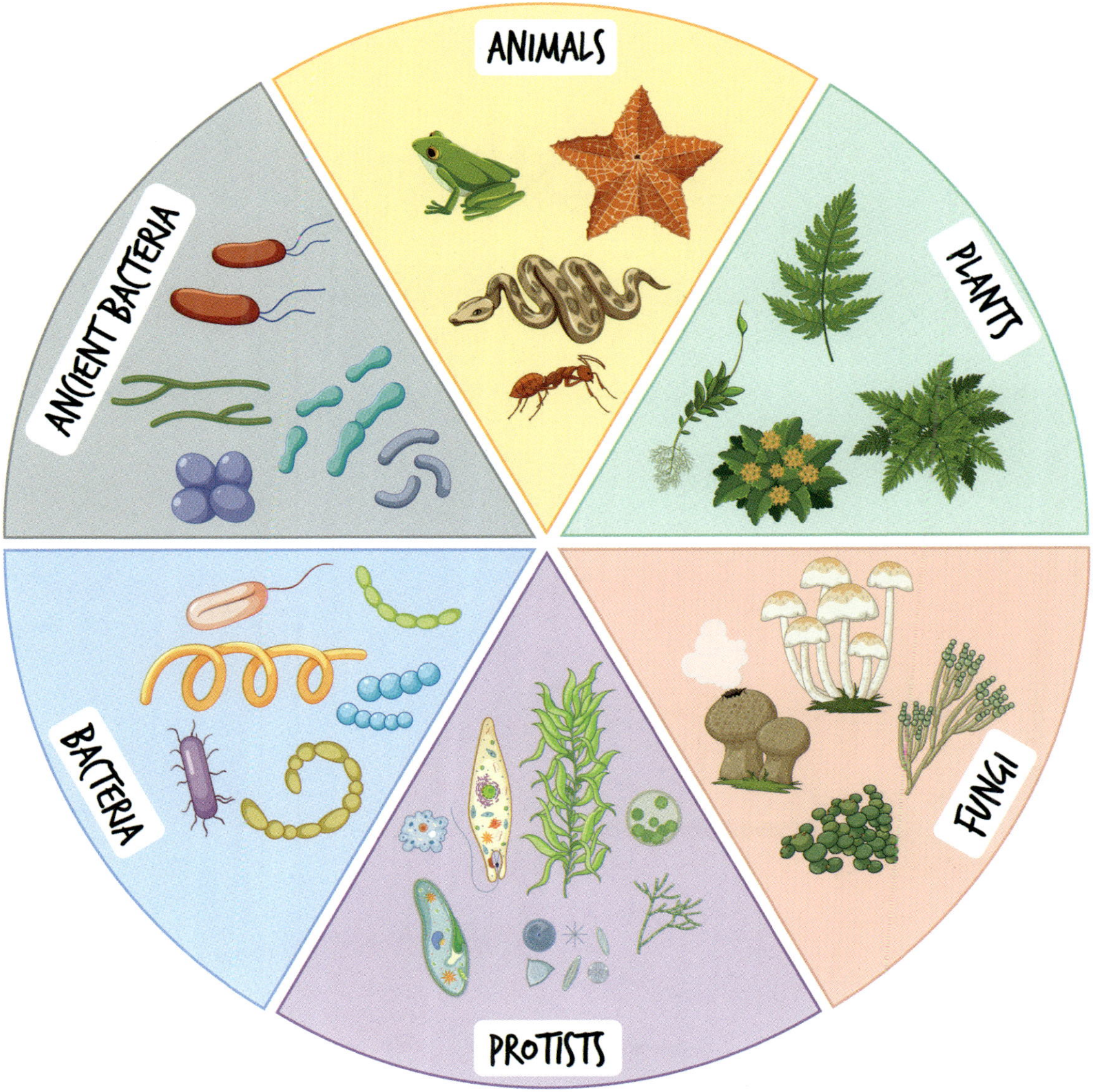

This diagram shows the six kingdoms of life, each of which are made up of cells.

WORD WISE

CELLS ARE THE BASIC UNITS OF LIFE THAT ARE RESPONSIBLE FOR ALL OF LIFE'S PROCESSES.

No Pulse

Nonliving things are not alive, and therefore don't carry out the life processes. However, not all nonliving things are the same. Some things, such as cars, cement, and metal, were never alive. Others, such as napkins, steak, and salad, were once living things.

This wooden desk is a nonliving thing made from a one-time living thing—a tree!

This necklace is made from metal, which was never alive.

Nonliving things can be grouped into two categories, or groups: natural things and **synthetic** things. Natural materials include those that are dug out of the ground, such as rocks, or the metals that we get from rocks. Synthetic things are materials made in factories, such as nylon and plastic.

WORD WISE

SYNTHETIC DESCRIBES A NONLIVING THING THAT WAS CREATED BY HUMANS AND NOT NATURALLY FOUND.

Helping Us

A nonliving thing doesn't need water, food, or sunlight to exist. It doesn't feed, grow, or reproduce because it isn't alive. However, living things rely on nonliving things. We use some nonliving things to make our lives easier or simply for pleasure. People play games on computers or with sports equipment, and we use machines to help us travel or do work.

Nonliving things help us to carry out life processes. Plants need light and water to make food. Animals need plants to get the nutrition they need. Living things must have air to breathe to release energy from their food. Living things would die without these nonliving things!

Nonliving things can make our lives easier!

compare and contrast

Which nonliving things do people need to survive? Which make their lives easier, but aren't necessary for their survival?

Certain nonliving things, such as air and water, allow us to survive.

Glossary

develop To grow.

environment Everything surrounding both living and nonliving things.

feces Poop.

fungus A decomposer, such as a mushroom, that lives off dead or decaying matter.

gecko A small lizard that lives in warm climates.

iguana A larger lizard that lives in tropical climates.

mammal An animal that gives birth to live babies and feeds their young milk from their body.

manatee A slow-moving underwater mammal. Manatees have been nicknamed "sea cows."

marsupial A mammal that has a tiny baby that develops in a pouch on its mother's body.

newt A small, brightly colored amphibian that lives in water and partly on land. A newt looks like a cross between a lizard and a frog.

physical Having to do with something's surroundings.

pincer The claw of a scorpion.

protist A single-celled microscopic organism that lives in water.

reaction Responding to something.

release To let go of.

respond To act or speak as a result of something that happened.

scorpion Small animals with a curved tail that can deliver a venomous sting.

unique Special and unlike others.

urine Pee.

For More Information

Books

Rivera, Andrea. *Living and Nonliving.* Minneapolis, MN: ABDO Zoom, 2018.

Simons, Lisa M. Bolt. *Is It Living or Nonliving?* North Mankato, MN: Pebble, 2022.

Spalding, Maddie. *Living vs. Nonliving.* Mankato, MN: The Child's World, 2021.

Websites

DK findout! What Is a Living Thing?
www.dkfindout.com/us/animals-and-nature/what-is-living-thing
Explore each of the seven life processes and their functions.

Firstcry: Living Things & Non-Living Things—Definition, Examples and Characteristics
www.firstcry.com/intelli/articles/living-and-non-living-things-definition-examples-and-characteristics
Learn more about the differences between living and nonliving things here.

Publisher's note to educators and parents: Our editors have carefully reviewed these websites to ensure that they are suitable for students. Many websites change frequently, however, and we cannot guarantee that a site's future contents will continue to meet our high standards of quality and educational value. Be advised that students should be closely supervised whenever they access the internet.

Index